SO-AIF-472

This book belongs to

_____

_____

PUFFIN BOOKS
Published by the Penguin Group
Penguin Group (NZ), 67 Apollo Drive, Rosedale,
North Shore 0632, New Zealand (a division of Pearson New Zealand Ltd)
Penguin Group (USA) Inc., 375 Hudson Street,
New York, New York 10014, USA
Penguin Group (Canada), 90 Eglinton Avenue East, Suite 700, Toronto,
Ontario, M4P 2Y3, Canada (a division of Pearson Penguin Canada Inc.)
Penguin Books Ltd, 80 Strand, London, WC2R 0RL, England
Penguin Ireland, 25 St Stephen's Green,
Dublin 2, Ireland (a division of Penguin Books Ltd)
Penguin Group (Australia), 250 Camberwell Road, Camberwell,
Victoria 3124, Australia (a division of Pearson Australia Group Pty Ltd)
Penguin Books India Pvt Ltd, 11, Community Centre,
Panchsheel Park, New Delhi – 110 017, India
Penguin Books (South Africa) (Pty) Ltd, 24 Sturdee Avenue,
Rosebank, Johannesburg 2196, South Africa

Penguin Books Ltd, Registered Offices: 80 Strand, London, WC2R 0RL, England

Originally published by Reed Publishing (NZ) Ltd, 2004
Reprinted 2005, 2007

First published in Puffin Books, 2008
10 9 8 7 6 5 4 3 2

Based on the Natural New Zealand ABC Wallchart by Helen Taylor © 2002
Copyright © Helen Taylor and Ben Brown, 2004

The right of Helen Taylor and Ben Brown to be identified as the authors of this work in
terms of section 96 of the Copyright Act 1994 is hereby asserted.
All rights reserved.

Printed in China through Bookbuilders, Hong Kong

All rights reserved. Without limiting the rights under copyright reserved
above, no part of this publication may be reproduced, stored in or
introduced into a retrieval system, or transmitted, in any form or by any
means (electronic, mechanical, photocopying, recording or otherwise),
without the prior written permission of both the copyright owner and
the above publisher of this book.

ISBN: 978 0 14 350316 3

A catalogue record for this book is available
from the National Library of New Zealand.

www.penguin.co.nz

NATURAL NEW ZEALAND

A B C

By Helen Taylor and Ben Brown

Aa
Albatross

Albatrosses are the biggest of all the seabirds. The royal albatross grows to over a metre in length, with a wingspan that can stretch to three and a half metres. Albatrosses spend most of their lives wandering the skies, often alone, above the vast Southern Ocean between New Zealand and Antarctica, soaring for days, even weeks at a time. They eat fish and squid and sleep on the sea. Maori call them toroa. They are the wanderers weeping for home. Taiaroa Head on the Otago Peninsula near Dunedin is the only mainland nesting colony of toroa in the world.

Maori call the bat pekapeka. This is a long-tailed bat. It lives in the forest fringes and at night it flits about using its tail a bit like a fishing net to catch insects. It spends the day sleeping in a hollow tree and hibernates in winter. There are three kinds of bat in New Zealand: long-tailed bats, short-tailed bats, and greater short-tailed bats. Both species of short-tailed bats are very rare.

Bb
Bat

Cc
Cabbage tree

If you look closely you can see that there is a cabbage tree on the moon. It was dragged there by Rona, in Maori mythology, when she scoffed and cursed at the moon one night. The moon came down and plucked her away, taking the cabbage tree she was clinging to with her. Cabbage trees can grow almost anywhere it seems! Washed-up trunks have been known to sprout on the shore. A burnt stump might shoot a new tree from its ashes. Maori often planted them as markers on a trail in pre-European times.

Dolphins seem to get along with human beings. Nine species of dolphin live in the waters around New Zealand. The Hector's dolphin is one of the smallest and rarest dolphins in the world, and is found nowhere else but in New Zealand. One Maori name for Hector's dolphin is Tutumairekurai — special ocean-dweller. Tutumairekurai are sometimes seen as guardian ancestors returned to look after us. It is said that only someone who has learnt great wisdom in his or her life might one day return as a dolphin.
The North Island Hector's dolphin is now called Maui's dolphin.

Dd
Dolphin

Ee
Eel

Eels live in nearly all New Zealand's waterways and lakes. The long-finned eel is a river dweller. It could, if it were lucky, grow to one and a half metres long over 50 or 60 years. Or at some point in its adult life it might join the great migration of eels in the thousands, down rivers and streams to the ocean where somewhere far off in the Pacific they spawn and die in the depths. But their offspring, as little eels called elvers, will make the journey all the way home and swim the same rivers in which their parents swam.

Ff
Frog

New Zealand has four species of native frog. They come out at night and have no croak. They have toes on their feet and they do not live in ponds but in forests, under rocks and stones. The native frog does not have tadpoles. It has 'froglets', little baby frogs with tails, which pop out of their eggs and onto their father's back. They are not very big, being little more than four centimetres long. All four species of New Zealand frog are very rare.

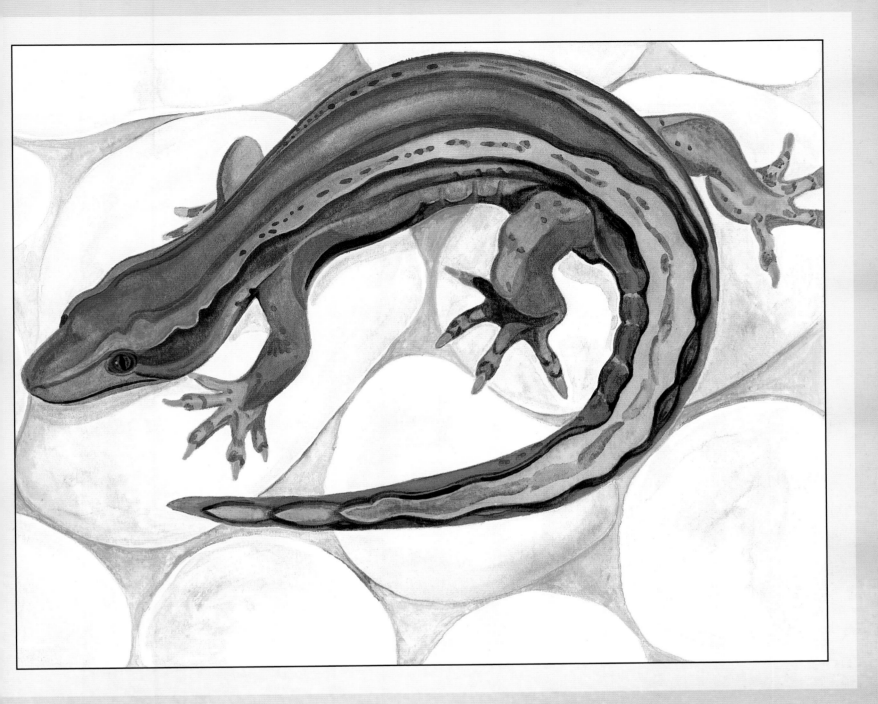

Geckos have five grippy toes on each foot. They do not blink. They can climb up anything, even glass. Some geckos bark, some of them chirp and others click. Geckos slip out of their old skins every six weeks. This is a goldstripe gecko, one of 29 native species of gecko in New Zealand. All of them are protected lizards. If you find a goldstripe gecko, don't catch it by the tail or it will leave the tail behind, wiggling in your fingers.

Gg
Gecko

Hh
Heron

There are few birds that seem more elegant than the white heron, or kōtuku. In New Zealand they nest only at Okarito on the West Coast of the South Island. Sometimes they can be seen from time to time in certain wetland and coastal areas round the country. Maori have a saying, Te kōtuku o te rerenga tahi, meaning The white heron of the single flight, as though it were a rare and special visitor who might not call again. To see one is said to bring good fortune.

Iceplants grow on the coast near the salty sea. They have to be tougher than they look because the coast can be a hard place for plants to live. Iceplants are a type of plant called a succulent. Succulent plants are very good at storing water. Their leaves feel spongy. Iceplants need to store water because of all the salt in the earth and air around them. Salt is very thirsty and will soak up water whenever it can.

Ii

Iceplant

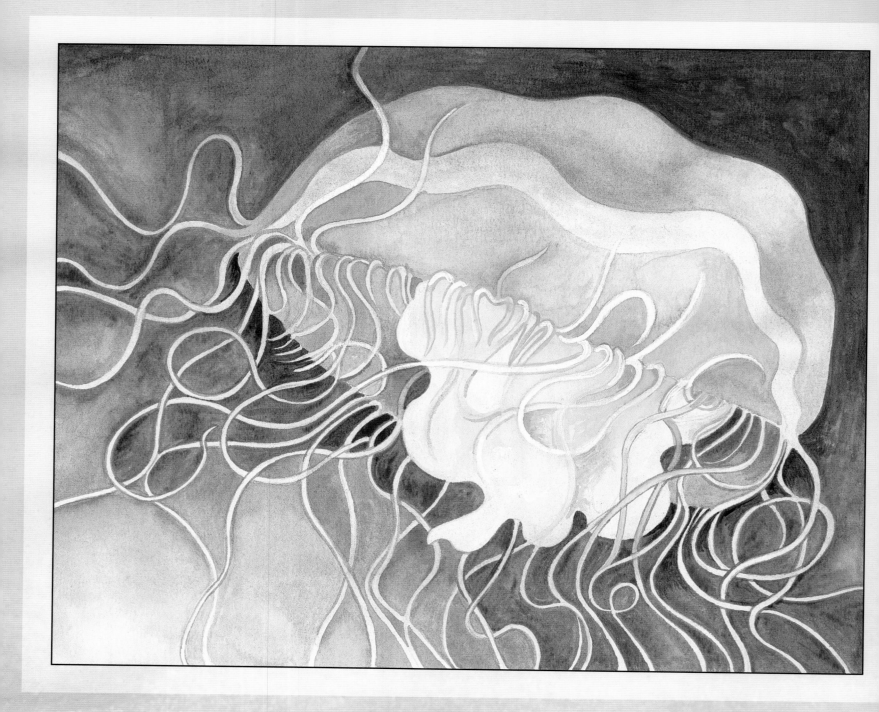

Jj
Jellyfish

Jellyfish seem to drift aimlessly through the water, but really they know where they are going as they pulse through the sea. Some jellyfish can grow to two metres across, with more than 20 metres of stinging tentacles drifting beneath them, colliding with tiny sea creatures that they eat. More often, though, they are a lot smaller. Jellyfish are common in New Zealand waters and are often seen in coastal swarms when the seas are warmer and food is plentiful.

T he kiwi is a popular symbol of New Zealand. There are six different kinds that live here but they are all becoming rare. This flightless bushwalker is unique in the world, all body and beak with warm shaggy feathers and stout legs with tough feet at the end of them for scratching in the forest litter. They are nocturnal, which means they get about at night. They are shy, elusive and secretive. The kiwi lays a remarkable egg, bigger in proportion to its body than any other bird, and the male kiwi will keep it warm in a burrow.

K k

Kiwi

Ll
Limpet

You may not think it, but a limpet gets around a bit. You usually see limpets clinging so tightly to a rock that they seem part of it. Their shell fits perfectly with the surface of the rock they are on. This is because wherever they wander over the rocks when the tide is in, limpets will always return to the exact same spot on the exact same rock where they started.

Maori call the morepork ruru. Ruru's eyes see everything in all directions. Maori have many songs and stories about this little New Zealand owl. The large paua-shell eyes of some Maori carvings are said to be the eyes of ruru. The call of a morepork can be thought of as an omen, sometimes good, sometimes not. These little birds of the night are skilful hunters. They are also bold creatures, and were often seen as guardians or protectors.

Mm
Morepork

Nn
Nikau

The nikau is New Zealand's only native palm tree, and it is the southernmost palm tree in the world. It grows mostly in the northern forests, especially where it's warmer, or in forests and groves along the northwestern coast of the South Island, but small stands also exist on Banks Peninsula, and even the Chatham Islands. Nikau palms can grow to 15 metres high and live for up to 300 years, perhaps more. They produce a mass of small red berries, which take nearly a year to ripen. Wood pigeons (kereru) love nikau berries.

According to one legend, Kupe discovered Aotearoa while chasing Te Wheke ā Muturangi (Muturangi's Octopus) across Kiwa's great ocean, which we call the Southern Pacific. The word octopus comes from two Greek words that together mean eight feet. An octopus is a remarkable creature. It can change colour according to its mood or surroundings. It can fit into seemingly impossible places. If it loses an arm (which is not uncommon) it will simply grow another. It has three hearts, while humans have to get by with one. Its favourite food is crayfish. If it is threatened, it disappears in a cloud of ink.

Oo

Octopus

Pp
Pūkeko

Pūkeko are characters. They are jaunty, inquisitive, cunning and bold. They can fly very well but they prefer not to. They can also swim but would rather walk. There are many Maori legends about pūkeko. In some stories they are thieves. In others they are noble. The red cap and beak are said to mark both good and bad, depending on which story you are listening to. Usually pūkeko like to graze and forage along the fringe-lands of swampy, marshy places, or along the banks and verges of rivers and streams, but they are adaptable. In fact whether city or swamp, country or town, you'll find a band of pūkeko there somewhere.

New Zealand's native koreke were once common on the tussocky grasslands and plains, especially in the South Island. They were hunted for food by Maori, and although they were easily caught, the fat little quails were always abundant. It wasn't until later settlers brought guns and dogs, and hunting quail became a sport, that koreke were threatened. Cats and ferrets also hunted quail, but the final straw was when settler fires turned grasslands and plains into paddocks and pastures. Koreke did not survive, and they were gone by the 1870s. The brown quail (pictured) was brought to New Zealand in the 1860s from Australia to increase quail numbers for hunting. This quail is still here today.

Qq
Quail

Rr
Raupo

Raupo was a wonderfully useful plant to Maori in the old days. Cakes were made from its pollen or, occasionally, a paste that was ground from its rhizomes. As a resilient wetland reed, its leaves had many uses. In bunches they could be made into thatching for the roofs of houses or they could be split, plaited, woven and tied to make baskets and mats plus many other things. The stalks of the raupo are strong and light enough to frame a kite, and sometimes they are used to make the decorated tukutuku panels that line the inside walls of carved houses.

New Zealand has over 1000 species of snail. This particular snail is found on the forest floor in the high hills round Nelson and Marlborough at the top of the South Island. It is very big, with a shell that can grow to more than 75 millimetres across. It lives in the dark and damp of the leaf litter where it ambushes giant earthworms for food. Some of those worms are over one metre long. Called ngata by Maori, snails are said to possess certain properties of healing.

Ss
Snail

Tt
Tuatara

The tuatara has been called a living fossil. This is because it is the only survivor of a group of reptiles that died millions of years ago. Strangely, it has a third 'eye' in the middle of its head that does not see but, rather, senses light. A tuatara looks like a lizard but it is not; it is a special reptile all on its own. Even so, it does lizard-like things. It sheds its skin, but only once or twice a year. It loses its tail if it is threatened, and a new tail will grow back. The word tuatara means 'peaks on the back' in Maori. Tuatara can live for a very long time, over a century perhaps, and they live only in New Zealand.

The umbrella fern is so named because it vaguely resembles an umbrella in the way that it spreads and hangs its leafy fingers — but don't bother trying to get out of the rain underneath one. Most of the world's 10,000 kinds of ferns grow in tropical places, which are hot and humid and often wet. New Zealand, though, is not tropical; it is temperate — not too hot, not too cold, and usually not too wet. So the 200 different kinds of ferns that are found in New Zealand have adapted well to live here.

Uu
Umbrella
fern

This vine is a rata vine and it is native to New Zealand. It grows up the trunk of a tall forest tree until it reaches the sunlight, where it forms branches and a small canopy of its own. When it does, the vine itself will lose its pretty little leaves, pull apart from the tree, and grow into a cable-like trunk. Other kinds of vines actually grow the other way round, starting in the treetop and growing down the trunk until it takes root in the ground, where it will, over time, become a tree itself, having first smothered the tree upon which it grew.

Vv

Vines

Ww
Weta

Weta Punga, also called the giant weta, is one of about 50 kinds of weta in New Zealand. Even though weta are found round the world, only New Zealand has as many different kinds or as many giants. In Maori mythology, Punga's children are the insects and creatures of the earth that were considered ugly. So this is Punga's weta. This one is a female. She has a long spike for a tail, which is really an egg-laying tube. In her life she might lay 400–500 eggs and grow to the size of a sparrow. That's a lot of weta!

There are many kinds of xymene in New Zealand. They live right round the coastline from the low-tide shore out to a depth of about 70 metres. Most are quite small, between five and twenty millimetres long, but some such as this one can grow to over six centimetres. Xymene can be found under rocks along the shoreline, or washed up on broad, sandy beaches. This is a female shell. It curls like a spiral staircase covered with dents, grooves and ridges. The male shell is smaller and smoother than this.

Xx
Xymene

Yy
Yellow-eyed penguin

This is the rarest penguin in the world. It is found on the southeast coast of New Zealand, parts of Stewart Island/Rakiura, and on one or two smaller islands south of New Zealand. As its name says, it has yellow eyes, unlike any other penguin. And as its Maori name, hoiho, suggests, it is a noisy shouter. Hoiho live alone, preferring a quiet burrow somewhere in a coastal forest to the usual crowds and colonies favoured by other penguins. It is the fourth largest of all the penguins, growing to over 60 centimetres tall, and can dive to depths of 100 metres.

Even though it is called a zigzag cockle this beautiful little shell is not a true cockle. It is really one of about 20 kinds of Venus shells living in New Zealand waters, buried in the sands of shore and seabed. They are slightly different in shape to cockle shells and, of course, are wonderfully patterned, which gives them their name. Maori call them Tawera after the morning star, which is really the planet Venus, and morning star is another name for this shell. Venus is the legendary Greek goddess of love. It is said that she was born in the sea.

Zz
Zigzag cockle

Not so long ago, Ben and Helen lived in a shack-like cottage near a swamp in the Motueka valley in the South Island of New Zealand. A marauding family of pukeko made regular forays into their garden, helping themselves to whatever they could carry away.

As an artist and illustrator, Helen found these vibrantly coloured rascals an irresistible subject and their antics seemed ideally suited to a story. The couple's first children's story, *The Thief of Colours*, was Ben's response to these antics.

Ben and Helen now live in Lyttelton with their two children, Connor and Sophie, where they continue to write and illustrate children's books.